This book belongs to

_____

LITTLE PEOPLE
■ IN ■
TOUGH SPOTS

Bible Answers for Young Children

V. Gilbert Beers
Ronald A. Beers

Illustrated by
Daniel J. Hochstatter

A division of
Thomas Nelson Publishers
Nashville

Published in Nashville, Tennessee, by Oliver-Nelson Books, a division of
Thomas Nelson, Inc., Publishers, and distributed in Canada by Lawson
Falle, Ltd., Cambridge, Ontario.

ISBN   0-8407-9157-7

Printed in Singapore

1 2 3 4 5 6 7 – 97 96 95 94 93 92

To Parents and Teachers

Today more than ever, our "little people," our children, are in tough spots, much tougher than we faced when we were children. We see this daily and want to help. We want to say in some unique, easy-to-understand way, "Others have been in tough spots, too, and it may help you to know what they did about it."

This is a book designed to relate Bible people and their down-to-earth problems to our children and their tough spots. Each situation starts with the child today, relates the tough spot they face to a Bible character and his or her problem, and then comes back to the child. Bible people of there and then relate to the child of here and now. This helps the child see life today in the context of the Bible and the Bible in the context of life today. We parents will see this, too, as we share it with our child.

—V. Gilbert and Ronald A. Beers

Contents

Have you ever felt like this boy? That needle looks ten feet long with teeth on it. But it isn't. Have you ever seen something that made you say, "I'm scared"? Perhaps it was a shadow, or a bully, or a needle like this, or something else.

But other people have been scared too. "Do you remember David when he fought Goliath?" Mother asks. "He must have been scared too. This is the way it happened."

One day the Philistines and Israelites went out to fight.

But the Philistines had a giant on their side. He was really big. And he had a big sword and spear and shield.

How could the Israelites fight him?

"I'll fight that giant!" David said. This seemed funny to some of the soldiers. David was not even as big as they were. But no one else would fight the giant. So what could they do but let David do it?

It must have looked strange to see someone pray before fighting a giant. But that's what David did.

"Wow! He's a lot bigger than I am," David thought. Do you think this made David scared?

"And look at all those things! All I have is my little slingshot."

"God will help me!"
David remembered.

Do you think David
stopped to thank God when
this happened? Would you?

"You're a brave boy," the doctor says.

"God helped me," the boy answers.

Next time you are afraid of something, remember David when he fought Goliath. And remember that God will help you too.

"I Have Too Much to Do"

Do you ever have too much work? Perhaps there are too many chores, or too much homework, or who knows what else? You feel like shouting, "I have too much to do."

But other people have too much work too. "Do you remember what happened to Noah?" a friend asks. "He had so much to do that it took him a hundred years and more to get his chores done. This is the way it happened."

One day God talked to Noah about His plans. "I will send a big flood," God told Noah. "Build a boat that will hold animals and birds and your family. Do it exactly the way I tell you." Noah began to cut wood and get it ready to build the boat.

Noah and his sons worked every day on the big boat. They worked for a year. They kept on working for many years. It took more than a hundred years to make this boat. But Noah wasn't through working yet.

Noah had to get food and water on board for all those animals. How would you like to feed a zoo for a year? That's what Noah had to do.

Now look what Noah has to do. There must be hundreds of animals and birds. Don't you wish you could help Noah? You can see how much work he has to do.

Of course it isn't easy to get a family ready for a big trip either. Have you ever gone on a trip for a year? It's a lot of work to get a family ready for a trip like that.

Do you suppose Noah ever said, "I have too much to do"? You would understand if he did, wouldn't you?

But there comes a time when we're glad we did our chores. Do you think Noah is glad for that now?

Do you think Noah is glad he did all of the work God told him to do? Do you think he is thanking God for telling him what to do? You would, wouldn't you?

Do you know what this girl is saying? "I'm glad I don't have to cut down trees and build a big boat and feed a zoo for a year and get my family ready for a big trip—all I have to do is my homework."

Do you think it's fun to finish your chores and homework so you can go outside to play?

And do you ever thank God for your chores? You should. They help to take care of your house and your family. And that's worth working for, isn't it?

"That Looks Like Fun"

"That looks like fun. Should I do it?" Have you ever said that when you see someone doing something that's not so good?

Other people have thought that too. "Do you remember when Moses' people had fun around the golden calf?" a friend asks. "This is the way it happened."

One day Moses went up onto a mountain. God wanted to give him some rules for the people.

Many days went by. But Moses did not come back. The people grew tired of waiting. "Moses will never come back," they said.

"Let's make an idol," someone said. "It will lead us instead of Moses and his God."

Moses' brother Aaron was in charge. "Bring your gold earrings," he ordered. Now you see what they are doing.

Before long, all those golden earrings became a golden calf. Moses wouldn't like this, would he?

Soon the people were dancing around the calf and doing things they should never do. But some of them didn't do this. "That looks like fun," they must have thought. "Should I do it?" But these people loved God, so they did not do what the others did.

Oh, oh! Now these people are going to be sorry for what they did. Do you see who is back?

Someone will be punished for this mess. Don't you think the people are sorry now for what they did?

Do you think this boy and girl are glad they did not do what the others were doing? Do you think those kids will be punished?

Do you know what will keep us from doing what we shouldn't do? Do you read your Bible each day? Do you pray each day? When you do, you won't do bad things, even when they look like fun, will you?

"Do I Have to Share?"

Do you like it when others share with you? Do you like to share with others? What if you are playing with some special toys? Sometimes you may want to ask, "Do I have to share?"

"Do you remember what David did?" a friend asks, "He had many things. He had good food. He had a beautiful palace. He had good clothes. He did not have to share these things. But he did. This is the way it happened."

One day King David was eating his good food. Or was he putting on his beautiful clothes? Or perhaps he was just sitting around in his beautiful palace.

"I want to share my good things," David thought. "I want to share them with Jonathan's children." Jonathan had been killed in a battle. Before that, Jonathan had been David's best friend.

"Are any of Jonathan's children alive?" David asked some friends.

"We don't know," they said. "But we will find out."

So these friends went here. They went there. They asked people about Jonathan's children. Then they came back to talk to King David.

"One of Jonathan's children is alive," they said. "He cannot walk well. He is crippled. His name is Mephibosheth." Would you like to be named Mephibosheth?

"Bring him here," said King David. So the friends went to find Mephibosheth. "The king wants to see you," they said. Mephibosheth was afraid. What would the king do to him?

Mephibosheth bowed down before King David. He was afraid of the king. "Please don't hurt me," Mephibosheth begged.

"I will not hurt you," said King David. "I want to share some of my good things with you. You will live in my beautiful house with me. You will have good clothes. You will eat good food."

Mephibosheth was so happy that King David shared with him. King David was happy too. He liked to share.

Would you like to be like King David? You can. The next time you are playing with toys and friends, ask what King David would do.

When you share your toys and things you will be happy. Your friends will be happy too. Next time they will want to share their toys with you.

"But I Wasn't Hurting Anyone"

Do people sometimes think you did something, but you didn't? Do people sometimes say, "It's his fault," or "She did it"? But you didn't do anything wrong. Sometimes you may want to shout, "But I wasn't hurting anyone. I didn't do anything wrong."

"Do you remember a wonderful man named Daniel?" a friend asks. "He tried to please God. He prayed. He talked with God. He also tried to be a good helper. He did many good things for his king. But some bad men tried to get him in trouble. This is the way it happened."

Daniel's king liked him very much. That's because Daniel was a good helper. He was also very wise. Daniel helped the king know what to do. He helped the king do good things.

But some other men did not like Daniel. They were jealous. They wanted Daniel's job. They wanted the king to like them instead of Daniel.

"We can't hurt Daniel," these bad men said. "But let's find a way to have the king hurt him."

So these bad men talked to the king. "People should pray to you," they said. "Make a new law. Anyone who prays to another god will be thrown into a lions' den." The king did not know that Daniel prayed to God each day. But these men did. They thought he would keep on praying, even if there was a new law. They were right.

Daniel kept on praying. Even hungry lions could not keep him from praying to God each day.

"Daniel prayed to his God," the men told the king. "You must throw him into a den of lions." The king was sorry he had made the law now. He knew these men had tricked him. He knew they wanted to hurt Daniel. He knew now that Daniel had done nothing wrong. It was these bad men who had done something wrong.

But the king had to do what his law said. He had Daniel put into a den of lions. These lions were hungry too. Do you think Daniel wanted to say, "But I wasn't hurting anyone"? God took care of Daniel. He made the lions keep their mouths shut. They couldn't eat Daniel.

The next morning the king took Daniel from the lions' den. He was happy that God took care of Daniel.

Then the king had the bad men thrown into the lions' den. Don't you think they were sorry they had tricked the king?

Would you like to be like Daniel? He kept on doing what pleased God, even when people said bad things about him. He kept on praying, even when he could have gotten hurt.

When you keep on doing what is right, people will believe you when you say, "I didn't do that. I wasn't hurting anyone."

"That's Mine!"

Have you ever wanted something that belonged to another boy or girl? Have you ever thought of taking it? Sometimes you may look at something a friend has and say, "That's mine!"

"Do you remember King Ahab?" a friend asks. "He wanted his neighbor's vineyard. But Naboth would not sell his vineyard. King Ahab wanted the vineyard even more now. He wanted to shout, 'That's mine!' This is the way it happened."

One day King Ahab walked outside his palace.
He walked past his neighbor's beautiful vineyard.
Ahab stopped to look at Naboth's vineyard. "What a
beautiful garden I could plant there," he thought.

Ahab thought he could see the beautiful garden.
He wanted Naboth's vineyard even more now.

That night King Ahab was like a spoiled little boy. He would not eat his dinner. He lay on his bed, pouting.

"What is wrong?" asked Queen Jezebel.

"I want Naboth's vineyard, but he will not sell it to me," said the king.

"I will get the vineyard for you," the queen said.

She had some bad men lie about Naboth. They said he cursed God and King Ahab.

Of course he had not done that.

Some other bad men took Naboth outside. They threw rocks at him until he died. "Now the vineyard is yours," Queen Jezebel told the king. The king was happy. He did not care that some people killed Naboth to get his vineyard.

Ahab almost ran to see his vineyard. He would tell everyone that it was his vineyard now. But God told His prophet Elijah what Ahab and Jezebel had done. "Tell them I will punish them," God said.

Elijah went to the vineyard. He saw Ahab standing there. "You have done something very bad," Elijah told Ahab. "God will punish you."

When you want to say, "That's mine!" remember King Ahab. When you want to take something that belongs to another boy and girl, don't do it! God punished Ahab for taking a vineyard that wasn't his.

It's much better to share. If you have something a friend wants, why not share it? Play together. If you want something a friend has, ask your friend to share. Do you think your friend will share?

"I'm Bigger Than He Is"

Have you ever had a new baby in your house? Perhaps when you looked at the new baby you thought, "I'm bigger than he is." But bigger isn't always better, is it?

Some of your friends are bigger or smaller or faster or slower or smarter or whatever.

But that doesn't make them better or worse than someone else. "Do you remember how the shepherds felt about Baby Jesus?" Father asks. "They didn't think they were better than Baby Jesus, did they? This is the way it happened."

Shepherds watched their sheep one night while Bethlehem was asleep.

You know how surprised the shepherds were when an angel began to talk to them. "God's Son has been born in Bethlehem," the angel told them.

Suddenly there were many angels in the sky. "Glory to God," they said. "Peace to men." "Let's go see Him!" someone said. You would want to do that, too, wouldn't you?

The shepherds almost ran to Bethlehem. They wanted to see God's Son, even though He was just a baby.

Do you suppose the shepherds thought, "I'm bigger than He is"? Do you suppose they thought Baby Jesus was not as important as they were because He was smaller?

The shepherds knew this little baby was God's Son. He was more important than they were, even though He was much smaller.

The shepherds told everyone they could about Jesus. They told them that God's Son had come as a little baby.

So it really doesn't matter if a friend is taller or shorter, or is fatter or skinnier, or has freckles or red hair or green eyes, or wears glasses or whatever, does it? These things do not make someone better or worse.

Aren't you glad that Jesus came as a baby? He could have come as a giant, or a rich man, or an important king. But He didn't. Perhaps He wanted to tell us that bigger, or richer, or taller is not really better.

"Do I Have to Give It Back?"

Did you ever want to take something that didn't belong to you? Did you take it? Some children take things that are not theirs. They know it is wrong to do this. Some don't want to keep what they take. They want to give it back. But others may ask, "Do I have to give it back?"

"Do you remember such a man who lived in Bible times?" a friend asks. "Zacchaeus took money from many people. He wanted to keep this money. Then one day he met Jesus. He knew what he had done was wrong. He must have asked then, 'Do I have to give it back?' This is the way it happened."

Zacchaeus was a tax collector. He made people pay money to him. He gave some of it to the Roman people who ruled the land. He kept much of it for himself.

People hated Zacchaeus. He worked for the Roman rulers and the people hated the Roman rulers. He was stealing from them. He was getting richer. They were getting poorer.

But one day Jesus came to Jericho, where Zacchaeus lived. Zacchaeus had heard many good things about Jesus. He wanted to see Jesus. He did not think Jesus would talk with such a bad person. But he wanted to hear what Jesus said.

But Zacchaeus was a short man. All the other people crowding around Jesus were taller. He could not get near Jesus. He could not even see Jesus as He talked with the people.

Then Zacchaeus had a good idea. He would climb a tree. He could see Jesus when He walked under the tree.

So Zacchaeus climbed the tree and waited. Jesus came under the tree. Zacchaeus was so glad that he could see Jesus now. He was glad that he could hear what Jesus said to the people.

Suddenly Jesus saw Zacchaeus sitting in the tree. He knew who Zacchaeus was. He knew how much the people hated Zacchaeus. But Jesus wanted to tell Zacchaeus how he could love God. "Come down from there, Zacchaeus," Jesus said. "I want to visit your house." Zacchaeus was so happy. Now he could ask Jesus many questions about God.

Jesus would help him please God.

Now Zacchaeus was sorry he had taken money from the people. He was ashamed. Zacchaeus must have asked, "Do I have to give it back?" Suddenly he knew what he must do. "I will give back everything I stole from people," he told Jesus. "I will even give back more than I stole."

So if you take something that doesn't belong to you, stop asking, "Do I have to give it back?" Remember Zacchaeus. Remember how he gave back everything he had taken.

If you give back something you took, perhaps the other boy or girl will want to share it with you. Do you think so?

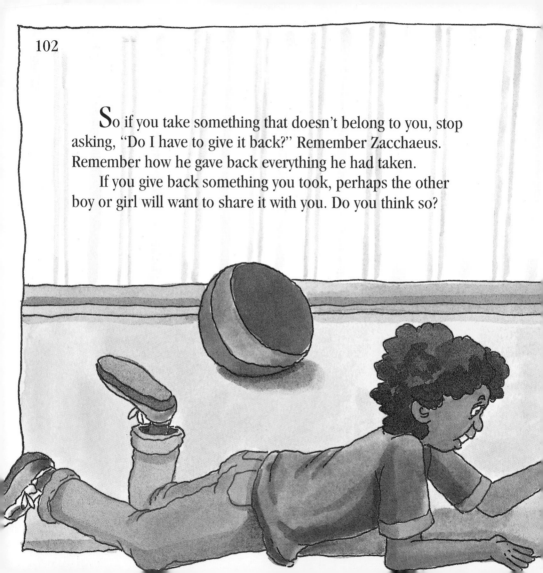

"There Won't Be Enough"

Sometimes Dads or Moms lose their jobs. Sometimes they don't have good jobs to lose. It's easy for someone in the family to worry about having enough money for food or clothing or other things. It's easy to say, "There won't be enough."

"Do you remember 5,000 hungry people in the Bible?" Father asks. "No one had food except one little boy. These people could have complained and said, 'There won't be enough.' But there was enough. There was even more than they needed. This is the way it happened."

A little boy went one day to hear Jesus talk. His mother thought he might get hungry, so she packed a lunch for the boy.

She put in five little loaves, like buns, and two little dried fish.

Don't you think it was a good idea to pack a lunch?

The little boy found a big crowd of people. Jesus was talking to them. So the boy sat down to listen to Jesus too.

Jesus talked a long time to the people. He talked until it was time for lunch.

Jesus' friends were worried. "Look at all these people," they said. "There are 5,000! What will we feed them? Nobody thought to bring lunch but one little boy. There won't be enough."

"There will be enough," Jesus told them. "There will be more than enough."

Jesus began to break the little loaves into pieces. He kept on breaking them. He also broke the little fish into pieces. He kept on breaking them too.

At last all 5,000 people had as much food as they wanted. They even had more than they could eat. There were 12 baskets of scraps left over. That's a lot of leftovers, isn't it?

The next time you or your family worry about having enough, remember Jesus and the 5,000. These people all had enough. Jesus helped them.

Be sure to pray about your problem. If Jesus can give 5,000 enough food to eat, He can help you and your family too.

"I Can't Talk About Jesus Here"

What do you say when a friend asks you about Jesus at a time like this? Do you think, "I can't talk about Jesus here"?

You're not the only one who has thought that. "Do you re-member what happened to Peter when he was ashamed to talk about Jesus?" a friend asks. "This is the way it happened."

Some religious leaders did not like Jesus. They were afraid the people would listen to Him instead of them. One night while Jesus was praying in a garden they sent soldiers to capture Him.

Peter was angry. He cut off the ear of one man with them.

Jesus put the man's ear on again. Then the soldiers took Jesus into Jerusalem. Peter followed to see what would happen.

The soldiers took Jesus to the high priest. He was the man in charge of the religious leaders. You can see what he wants to do to Jesus.

Peter wants to be near Jesus. These people are not his friends, but he sits down with them to keep warm.

"You are one of Jesus' friends," a woman said. Peter was afraid. "I can't talk about Jesus here," he thought. So Peter cursed and said he didn't even know Jesus.

But do you see who heard Peter? Do you think Peter is ashamed and sorry that he said what he did?

You can see how sorry Peter is now. Do you think he wants to tell people about Jesus from now on?

Peter became a great preacher. He told thousands about Jesus. He never, never said, "I don't know Jesus" again. Would you like to be like Peter?

Now what do you think this boy is saying? Some people will laugh when we tell them about Jesus. Some will not listen. But some will listen and become Jesus' friends.

Would you like to tell someone about Jesus today? Would you like to tell that person that Jesus is your friend? Do you think Jesus will be pleased if you do?

"Will Someone Help Me?"

Do you ever get into trouble? Perhaps it is something you do, or something you don't do. Or you may meet someone who isn't very friendly. At a time like this, you want to say, "Will someone help me?"

But other people get into trouble too. "Do you remember what happened to Paul at Damascus?" a friend asks. "He got into big trouble when he told people about Jesus. This is the way it happened."

Before Paul met Jesus he was a mean man. His name then was Saul. He put Jesus' friends in jail and got them into lots of trouble.

Saul, or should we just call him Paul,

got worse. He kept on getting Jesus' friends into trouble. He even went to Damascus to hurt them. But on the way Jesus had a little talk with Paul. "That's enough!" He said. "Stop hurting My friends and start helping them."

Jesus wanted to be sure that Paul would listen. So He made the light from heaven so bright that Paul couldn't see for awhile. That's why these men are leading Paul into Damascus.

Paul did listen to Jesus. Now he knew that Jesus was God's Son. He knew also that Jesus wanted him to help Him. So Paul began to tell people in Damascus that Jesus was God's Son.

Now Paul is in trouble. You can see that. These men want to hurt him or even kill him. Do you suppose Paul asked, "Will someone help me?"

"We will help you," Paul's friends said. "We will get you out of trouble." Do you see how they plan to do that?

That's what good friends do. When we're in trouble, they help us. Remember that when your good friend is in trouble too. And remember that Jesus will help your friends to help you.

"Thank you! Thank you!" Paul said. He is glad for good friends who help. Now he will remember to help other friends who get into trouble.

Aren't you glad for good friends to help you when you need them?

Don't forget to say "thank you" when good friends help you out of trouble. And don't forget to say "thank you" to Jesus too.

"Nobody Wants to Listen to Me"

Have you ever thought, "Nobody wants to listen to me"? Sometimes even our best friends don't listen, do they? Sometimes we think Mother or Father aren't listening. Then we want to shout, "Nobody wants to listen to me."

"Do you remember a Bible-time man named Paul?" a friend asks. "He wanted to tell people why he loved Jesus. He wanted people to listen to him. But many didn't. He could have shouted, 'Nobody wants to listen to me.' This is the way it happened."

One day Paul came to Jerusalem. He wanted to talk to God in His house. But some men hated Paul. They hated him because he loved Jesus.

They did not want him telling people about Jesus. They didn't want to listen to Paul. And they didn't want others to listen to him, either.

These men grabbed Paul. They shouted to their friends to help capture him. They wanted to kill him. But some soldiers took Paul from the men. By this time there was a big crowd of people.

"May I speak to these people?" Paul asked the soldiers. Paul wanted to tell them why he loved Jesus. But when Paul spoke to the people they became angry. Paul must have thought, "Nobody wants to listen to me."

Paul tried to talk with some of the leaders of the people. Some were called Pharisees. Others were called Sadducees. Paul said some things the Pharisees liked. But these same things made the Sadducees angry.

Before long, there was a big argument. The Pharisees and the Sadducees were quarreling because of Paul. Again, Paul must have thought, "Nobody wants to listen to me."

Paul was put into prison in a city called Caesarea. He talked with a governor. He told the governor why he loved Jesus. But the governor put him back into prison. He talked with another governor and told him why he loved Jesus. But he put Paul back into prison too.

Paul even talked with a king and told him why he loved Jesus. But he was put back into prison again. Paul must have thought, "Nobody wants to listen to me." Would you have stopped telling people about Jesus? Paul didn't. He kept telling people about Jesus. He kept telling people why he loved Jesus.

So the next time you think nobody wants to listen, remember Paul. Paul kept on telling people about Jesus, even when it seemed that nobody wanted to listen. If you want to talk with your parents or friends, keep on trying. If you want to tell others about Jesus, keep on trying.

Some people really do want to listen to you.

152

THOMAS NELSON PUBLISHERS
Nashville, Tennessee
Printed in Singapore